How to Art Doodle

Simple

Pattern

Building Techniques

Carolyn Scrace

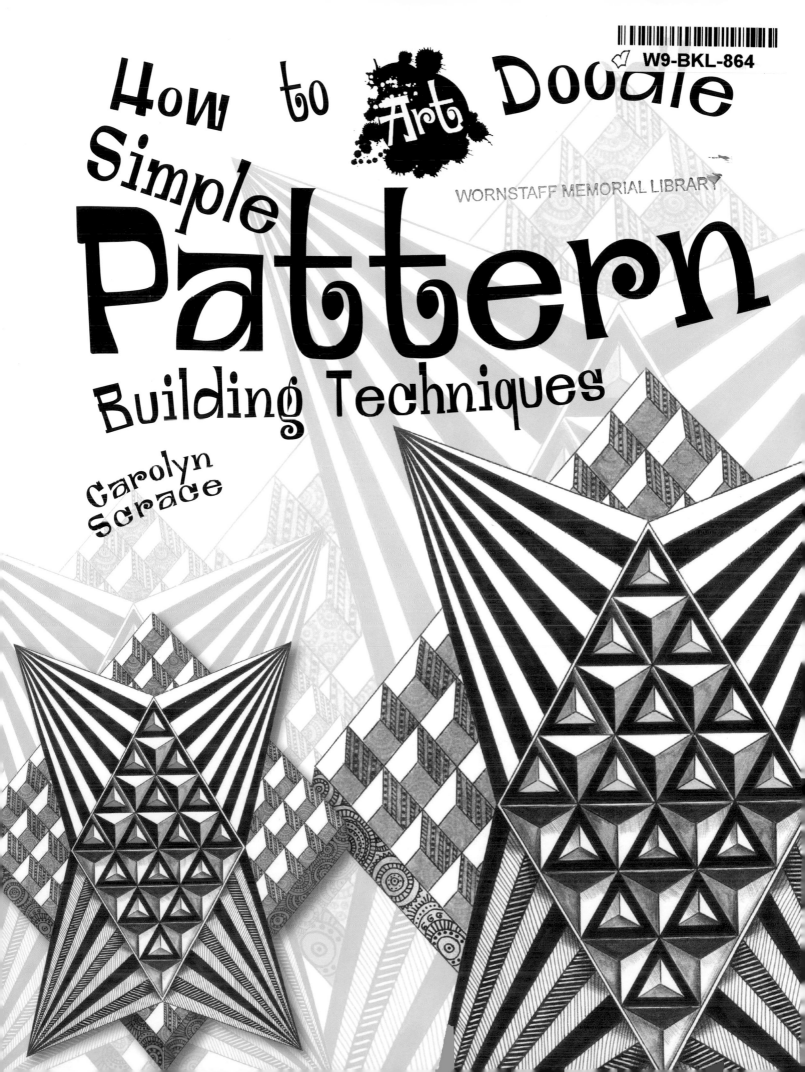

This edition first published in MMXV
by Book House
Reprinted in MMXVI

Distributed by Black Rabbit Books
P.O. Box 3263
Mankato
Minnesota MN 56002

© MMXV The Salariya Book Company Ltd
Printed in the United States of America.
Printed on paper from sustainable forests.

Cataloging-in-Publication Data is available
from the Library of Congress

HB ISBN: 978-1-909645-50-9
PB ISBN: 978-1-910184-36-3

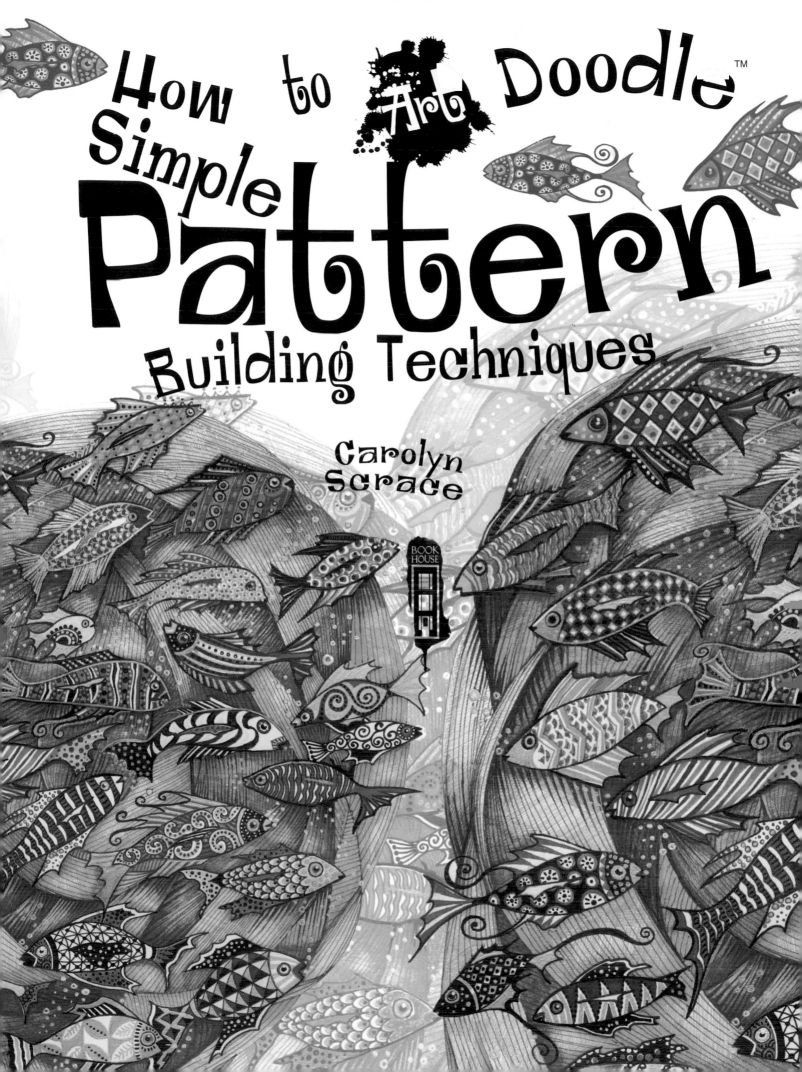

How to Art Doodle™

Simple Pattern

Pattern

Building Techniques

Carolyn Scrace

BOOK HOUSE

Contents

Please note: Sharp blades and scissors should be used under adult supervision.

Introduction

Art Doodling releases creativity and develops drawing skills. Discover the thrill of using simple shapes and lines to build up complex patterns. Learn to compose inspiring images and to develop exciting techniques for Art Doodling.

Do it anywhere!

Art Doodling patterns can be done anywhere, and need no special equipment. An old pencil stub and a scrap of paper is all that you need!

World full of patterns

Patterns surround us, they are everywhere we look—on buildings, clothes, furnishings, packaging—the list goes on! Explore the inspiring patterns found in the world of nature!

Sketchbook

Keep a small sketchbook or notepad with you at all times! Collect patterns and make notes to refer back to any time you get stuck for ideas. Use it like a scrap book and stick in pieces of old lace and fabric, dried flowers and leaves, photographs and magazine cuttings.

Deconstructing

Some patterns might appear too complex to doodle. Learn to break patterns down into their main components and simple shapes and before long you will be designing your own incredible Art Doodle patterns.

Breaking down patterns

Deconstruct an Art Doodled pattern (castle—left):

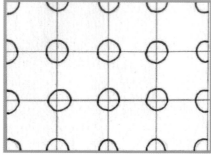

1. Pencil in a grid. Ink in circles (as shown).

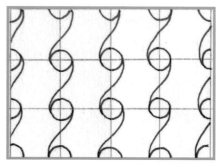

2. Link the circles vertically using curved ink lines.

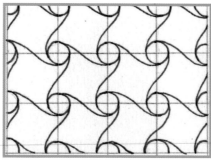

3. Repeat the curved lines horizontally.

4. Add pencil shading.

Deconstruction of the balloon pattern (right):

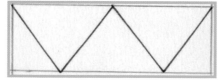

1. Ink in two horizontal lines and zigzag lines.

2. Add lines to the zigzag (as shown).

3. Add more lines on top (as shown).

4. Add black and red patterns.

Deconstructions of two more patterns (castle—left):

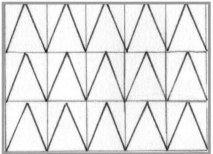

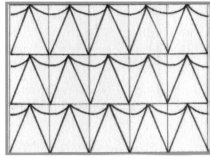

1. Pencil in a grid. Ink in a zigzag line.

2. Add horizontal lines and curved lines.

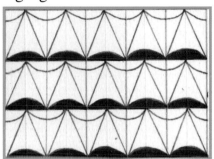

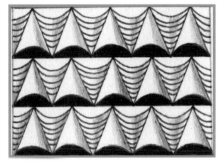

3. Add more curved lines and fill the shape with black.

4. Add curved stripes and pencil shading.

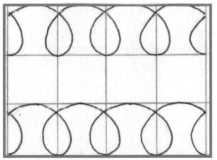

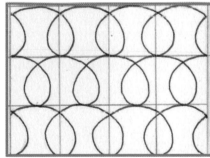

1. Pencil in a grid. Ink in curly lines (as shown).

2. Draw in more curly lines (as shown).

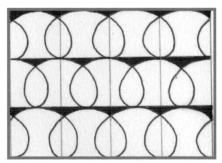

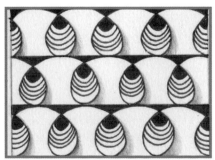

3. Ink in horizontal lines and fill in with black.

4. Add curved stripes and fill in with black (as shown). Add pencil shading.

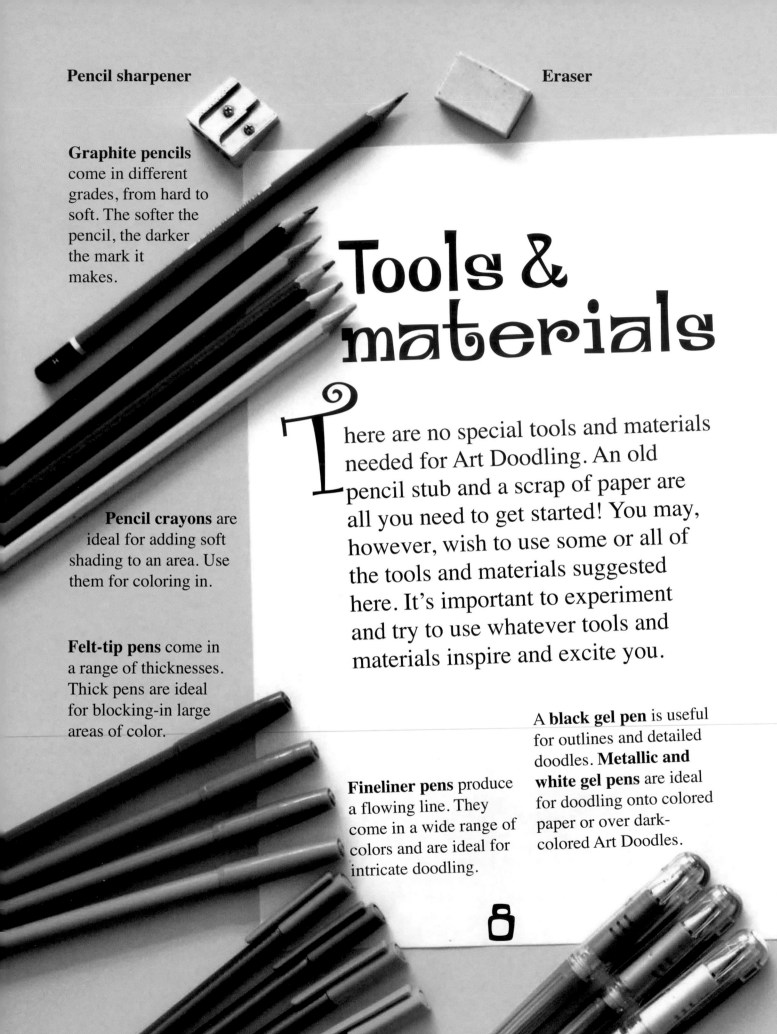

Pencil sharpener

Eraser

Graphite pencils come in different grades, from hard to soft. The softer the pencil, the darker the mark it makes.

Pencil crayons are ideal for adding soft shading to an area. Use them for coloring in.

Felt-tip pens come in a range of thicknesses. Thick pens are ideal for blocking-in large areas of color.

Tools & materials

There are no special tools and materials needed for Art Doodling. An old pencil stub and a scrap of paper are all you need to get started! You may, however, wish to use some or all of the tools and materials suggested here. It's important to experiment and try to use whatever tools and materials inspire and excite you.

Fineliner pens produce a flowing line. They come in a wide range of colors and are ideal for intricate doodling.

A **black gel pen** is useful for outlines and detailed doodles. **Metallic and white gel pens** are ideal for doodling onto colored paper or over dark-colored Art Doodles.

8

Ruler

Thick-tipped marker pens are perfect for filling in large areas. Fine-tipped, **permanent marker pens** are great for outlines and adding detail.

Types of paper

Cartridge paper comes in a variety of weights. Heavyweight paper is good for water-based paint. Note: Ink lines may bleed or run on some cartridge papers.

Bristol board or **paper** may be textured or smooth. Smooth **Bristol board** is good to work on with pencils, pencil crayons, markers, felt-tips, gel pens, and fineliner pens for adding fine details.

Sketchpad for jotting down ideas and trying out designs.

Use your sketchbook for experimenting with new techniques and keep notes of what materials you used.

felt-tip and fineliner

Palette (or clean saucer) for mixing paint.

Paintbrushes come in a wide range of sizes.

Colored inks and **watercolor** paints are ideal for covering large areas of a design with subtle color.

Gouache is opaque watercolor. Use it for painting areas with plain, flat color.

9

Inspiration!

Fruit and vegetables come in all different shapes and sizes, and make wonderfully inspiring sources for pattern designs.

Keep it simple!

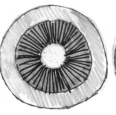

To create a pattern design, study the shape of a fruit or vegetable.

Start by drawing very simplified versions of the fruit and vegetables.

Pattern repeat

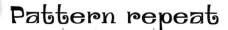

First draw a grid. Trace your design and, using the grid, line up each image.

To create free-flowing patterns, trace your design randomly.

Now design your Art Doodle using these patterns. Varying the size of the different elements of your design will make it more vibrant.

11

Flotilla

These simple boats make ideal shapes to Art Doodle. First try drawing the patterns below by following the step-by-step guides. Then use some of your own fantastic designs to create a flotilla of fabulous sailing boats!

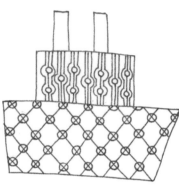

1. Draw a boat shape. Add lines and dots (as shown).

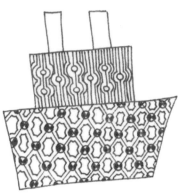

2. Add circles and more lines (as shown).

3. Add even more lines (as shown).

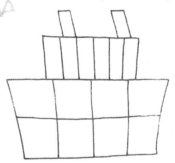

1. Draw a boat shape. Add lines (as shown).

2. Draw in circles and zigzag lines (as shown).

3. Add more lines, dots, and black triangles (as shown).

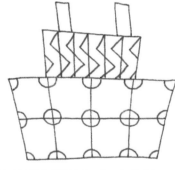

1. Draw a boat shape. Add lines (as shown).

2. Add spirals and zigzag patterns (as shown).

3. Add more lines and black triangles (as shown).

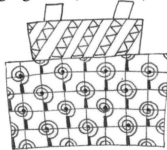

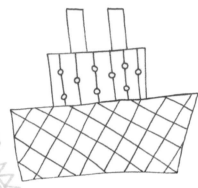

Draw a selection of different-shaped boats.
Draw in wavy ocean lines. Use bright,
contrasting colors to Art Doodle the boat
patterns. Doodle the waves using blue
fineliner and silver gel pen.

13

Fabulous fish

Coral reefs are teeming with beautifully colored fish covered with incredible patterns! Draw an underwater scene and fill it with fish decorated with your own fabulous designs!

Keep it simple!

1. Draw a fish shape. Draw a curved grid onto the fish's body (as shown).

2. Add curved, diagonal lines (as shown). Draw in a zigzag line down the tail.

3. Continue adding more lines (as shown). Start coloring in the patterns.

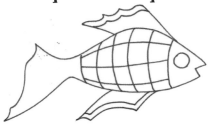

1. Draw a fish shape. Add thin, black, vertical stripes.

2. Color in orange and red stripes (as shown),

3. Add black and gold to finish the patterns (as shown).

Composition

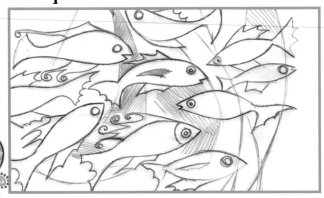

1. Pencil in a rough oval shape, then fill it with little fishes.

2. Ink in the pencil lines using blue fineliner pen. Indicate the water pattern using fine, parallel lines.

14

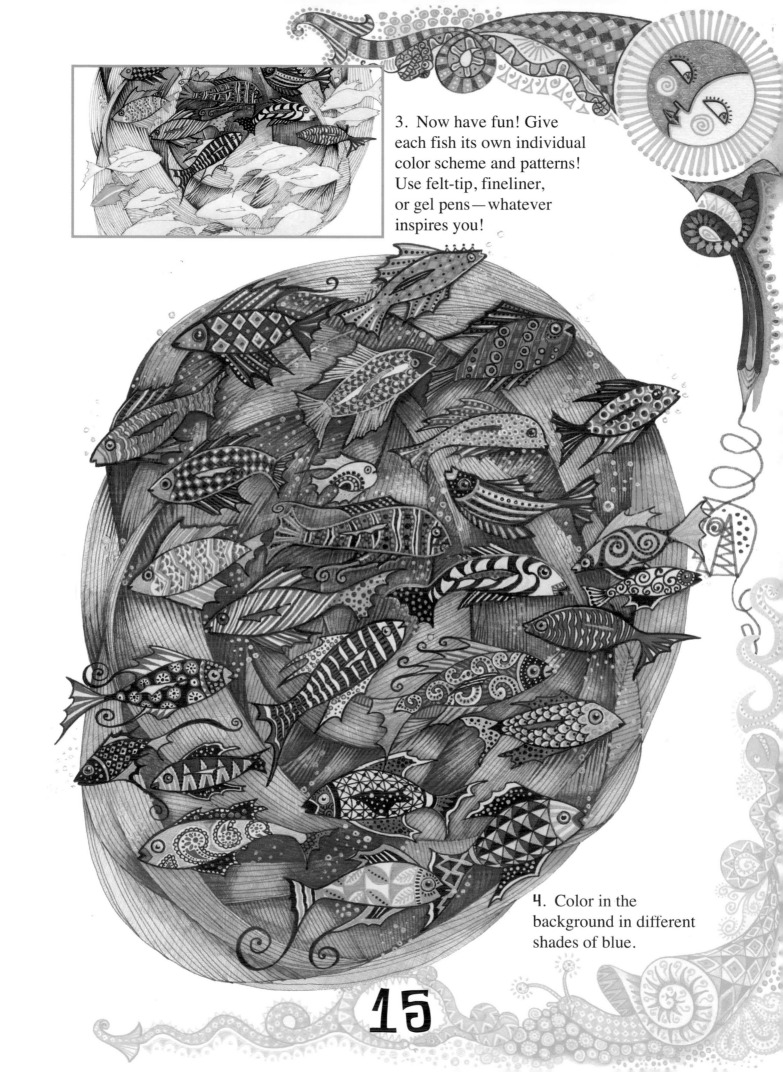

3. Now have fun! Give each fish its own individual color scheme and patterns! Use felt-tip, fineliner, or gel pens—whatever inspires you!

4. Color in the background in different shades of blue.

15

Using templates

It's great fun drawing around templates and Art Doodling patterns into the shapes you've created. Draw around your hand, add a head and arms to each digit, then design a set of wacky characters to doodle!

1. Do some rough sketches of your ideas. Draw around your hand, then try sketching in some "finger"people!

2. When you are happy with your design, redraw it in pencil onto a fresh sheet of paper.

3. Go over the pencil lines with black fineliner pen. Once the basic shapes are drawn, start adding areas of pattern.

4. Use fineliner pens and felt-tip pens to add color. Some patterns work best if the white of the paper is part of the design.

5. Experiment by laycring dark colors on top of light colors and then add doodling.

Artist's tip: Try tracing the shape of your hand then add doodling to the shape around it instead.

Fantasy...

Free your imagination and create a magical world of castles and strange flying machines! Use a bold, simple design then fill large areas with Art Doodle patterns. For added impact use black and white for the background and restrict color to one main area.

1. Make thumbnail sketches and experiment with your compositions.

2. Pencil in your finished design. Starting with the main image, ink over the pencil lines with black fineliner pen. Block in areas of color.

3. Begin Art Doodling the balloon. Contrasting bands of solid black next to yellow and red doodling attract attention and add impact to the design.

Turn to pages 6, 7, and 22 for helpful pattern guides.

4. Ink in the rest of the flying machine. Leave the fuselage white so that it stands out against the background. Use black fineliners to Art Doodle the castle, hills, and sky.

5. Add pencil shading to bring parts of the design forward and push other parts back.

Using tone

Tone refers to the lightness or darkness of an area. Tone varies from brilliant white through every shade of gray to deep black. Artists use tone to make objects appear three dimensional and to add depth and atmosphere to an image.

1. Make rough sketches of your design ideas. Choose a light source so that the dark areas of your design are consistent. Add shade to areas using a pencil and ballpoint pen hatching.

Doodling!

Turn to page 22 for a step-by step guide to drawing and doodling two of the following 3D pattern designs.

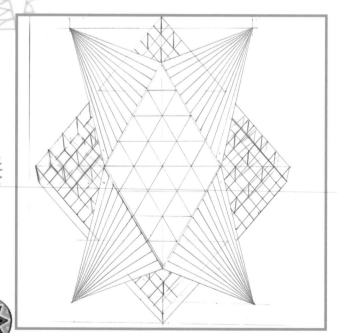

2. Pencil in your design. Use a ruler and take your time. Start by drawing the central diamond shape, then work outwards.

3. Ink in the pencil lines with black fineliner pen. Block in the black, red, and gray areas with fineliner and felt-tip pens. Erase any pencil marks.

4. Art Doodle light gray areas with dark gray doodles, and pale gold areas with golden brown doodles.

Light source

5. Add black ball-point pen or pencil shading to reinforce the 3D effect!

21

Pattern builder

These step-by-step examples show how to Art Doodle some of the patterns used in this book.

Using tone (Pages 20-21)

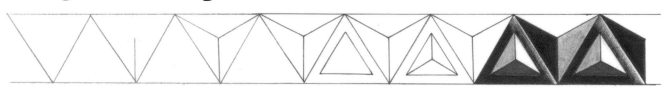

1. Draw parallel lines, then a zigzag. Draw three short lines centered on alternate triangle shapes (as shown).

2. Draw a smaller triangle inside the remaining shapes. Repeat the three line pattern inside (as shown).

3. Color in using pale gold, red, black, and gray. Add shading (as shown).

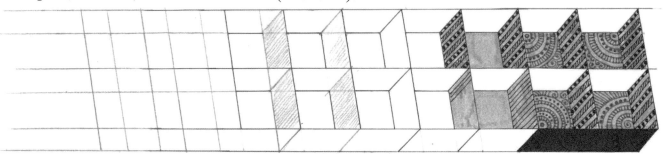

1. Pencil in horizontal lines as shown then add angled lines to create an asymmetric grid.

2. Draw short diagonal lines (as shown). Lightly shade in gray shapes as you work to check the pattern is correct.

3. Ink in the pencil lines. Color in with pale gold, red, and gray. Add simple doodle patterns (as shown).

Fantasy... (Pages 18-19)

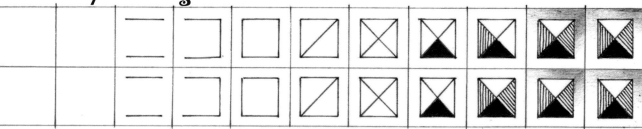

1. Ink in a grid. Add short horizontal lines.

2. Add vertical lines to make square shapes. Draw a cross in each square.

3. Ink in the bottom triangle. Add black stripes and pencil shading (as shown).

Glossary

3D three-dimensional.

Asymmetric not matching on either side of a center line.

Background area behind an object or image.

Blocking-in laying down areas of flat color.

Color scheme a planned combination of colors used in an artwork.

Composition how an artist arranges shapes, sizes, and colors, the different elements that make a piece of art.

Contrasting colors those that create the strongest contrasts such as red and green, blue and orange, yellow and violet.

Deconstructing breaking down into basic steps or components.

Design a graphic representation, usually a drawing or a sketch.

Flotilla a fleet of ships or boats.

Fuselage the main body of an aircraft.

Hatching a series of fine, parallel lines, a shading technique.

Layout an arrangement, plan, or design.

Light source the direction of light.

Proportion the size, location, or amount of one part of an image in relation to another.

Rough a quick sketch of the main elements in a picture.

Shading the lines or marks used to fill in areas or represent gradations of color or tone.

Sketch a preparatory drawing.

Technique an accepted method used to produce something.

Template a pattern used for making many copies of a shape.

Three-dimensional having, or appearing to have, the dimension of depth as well as width and height.

Thumbnail sketches usually very small, quick, abbreviated drawings.

Tone the lightness or darkness of an area.

Index